A   O

The
Holy Sacrifice
of
The Mass

Priests Edition

The HOLY SACRIFICE

OF

The MASS

Priests Edition

FOREWORD

This book is written to act as a manual for the proper movements and conduct for the celebration of Holy Mass. It incorporates liturgies from Latin tradition, but also adapts more inclusive roles for the faithful to act as priest-participants interceding for the whole human family before God. This first volume goes into the Mass(es) step by step for the Leader-Priest. The simple step by step format with footnotes on the symbolism and purpose of the movements help in cultivating a mystical experience for the celebrant full of illumination.

Table of Contents

Foreword.. 2

Vesting Prayers 4

Colors of the Liturgical Seasons 8

The Solitary Mass (Altar arrangement) 11

The Private Rite 13

The Holy Mass (Public Rite from Novus Ordo) 51

Appendix 101

Mass Clock **118**

A Prayer Before Mass (& Solitary Rite of Confession) 119

Important Prayers **124**

3

VESTING PRAYERS

If anything is taken off: "Take off and put away from me O' Lord my former sins, and create me a new person in You."

Hygenic Hand washing: "Bestow virtue upon my hands O' Lord, that I may serve you in purity as do your holy angels."

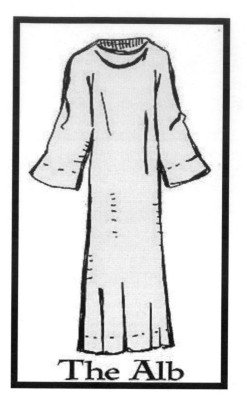

Fig.1

The Alb: "Wash me O' Lord and cleanse my heart, that with those who have washed their robes in the Blood of the Lamb, I may rejoice eternally with you."

The Cincture

Figure 2

The Cincture: "Gird me about O' Lord with the belt of Faith and guard my chastity, extinguish all uncleanness within me that the power of purity shall abide in me".

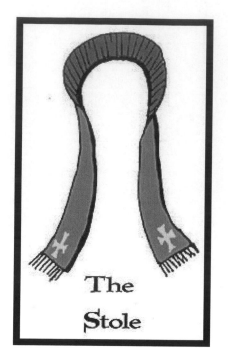

The Stole

Fig. 3

The Stole: "O' Jesus, the Good Shepherd, restore unto me the stole by means of which we are led to Life Everlasting, lost through the first sin. Though unworthy, thus adorned may I humbly approach Thine altar to celebrate Holy Mass and praise Thee in Heaven eternally with Thy Saints".

The Chasuble

Figure 4

The Chasuble: "Lord Jesus, You said your yoke is easy and your burden light, grant that I may bear it in joy and administer worthily the abundance of your mercy and grace to your people".

6

Colors of the Liturgical Seasons

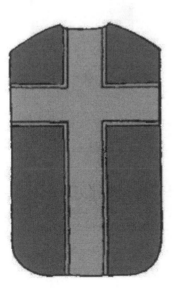

Fig. 5

Green: Used for times between major feasts, and solemnities
symbolizing the daily life of the Church.

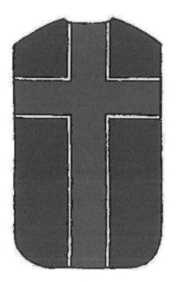

Figure 6

Violet: In service during Advent (the month before Christmas) and
Lent (7 weeks before Easter). Also Funerals and supplication.

Fig. 8

Red: Solemnities of Holy Week, Pentecost, the feast days of Apostles
and Martyrs. Advised for Masses of Exorcism.

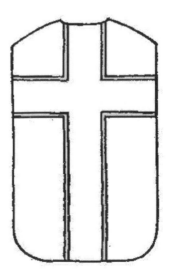

Fig. 9

White: The earliest liturgical color. Employed during Christmas and
Easter, all solemnities of The Trinity, Christ, Mary and saints who
are not martyrs (confessor-saints). Weddings, Baptisms also
make use of white. Use for blessing rituals.

8

Figure 10

Pale Rose: The color associated with joy and happiness. Traditionally signifying the journey time to Bethlehem at the first Christmas, and the final journey of Christ to Jerusalem; both journeys important to the redemption of mankind. Respectively these are the fourth week of Advent and two weeks before Easter. Funerals of children.

Fig. 11

White with Blue accent: Feasts of The Virgin Mary.

Figure 12

Black and/or Grey: Used for Funerals, All Souls Day, Masses for
the Deceased. Good Friday Solemnity. Not
advised for Extreme Unction rites or for
Exorcisms.

10

✠ The Solitary Mass ✠

This Mass is patterned after the Latin rite and is intended for Priests who due to certain circumstances, must celebrate alone or not at all. This conforms to the guidelines in the General Instructional of Roman Missal.

Appointing the Altar:

The Altar should at least be 30 inches by 48 inches and waist high. An altar stone should be obtained for the Chalice to rest on. Traditionally, these hold the relics of martyrs who died for their faith in Christ. It is not essential, but best for portable altars of wood. It should have linens or cloths draped upon it. White is mandatory, but this may overlay a liturgical color of the season. The following pages are an accounting of all that should be present on the altar for the celebration of Holy Mass.

Necessary Items:

1. Altar Linens

10. Chalice Veil

2. Crucifix

3. White Candles

4. Corporal Cloth

5. Chalice

6. Purificator Cloth

7. Paten with Host

8. Pall cover of Paten and Chalice

9. Burse which holds the Corporal

11. Ciborium which holds the host(s)

12. Wine & Water Cruets

13. Water Flagon for ritual washing

14. Lavabo bowl for washing hands

15. Hand Towel

16. Holy Water and Asperge

17. Mass Book of the Holy Liturgy

18. The Holy Bible for readings or
    Lectionary

12

The Private Rite

The Introductory Rites:

Stand a short distance from the Altar, pray for a moment and begin:

Make the sign of the Cross ~~ *and Say*

In the name of The Father, The Son, and The Holy

Spirit. Amen.
I will go to the altar of God, my God Who renews my
spirit.

13

Do Me Justice, O God, and fight my fight against
a faithless world; rescue me from the wicked and
deceitful.

Pray the Confiteor:
I confess to Almighty God,
To Blessed Mary Ever Virgin,
To Blessed Michael the Archangel,
To Blessed John the Baptist,
To the Holy Apostles Peter And Paul,
To All The Saints, And to You, O Christ,
That I Have Sinned Exceedingly in

Thought, Word, And Deed,
(Strike the Chest Three Times)
Through My Fault, Through My Fault,

Through My Most Grievous Fault.

Therefore I Beseech Blessed Mary Ever

Virgin,

Blessed Michael The Archangel,

Blessed John The Baptist,

The Holy Apostles Peter And Paul,

All The Saints, and You O Christ,

To Intercede To The Lord Our God For Me.

14

(Bow your head slightly toward the altar)

May Almighty God Have Mercy On Us, Forgive
Us Our Sins, And Bring Us To Life Everlasting.
Amen.
May The Almighty and Merciful Lord Grant Us

✠

Pardon,   Absolution, And Remission Of Our Sins.
Amen.   (Make the Sign of the Cross)

(Draw near, bow down and kiss the altar or altar stone)

Pray:

Take away my sins, I pray you O Lord, so that with pure mind I may worthily enter the Holy of Holies, and by the merits of the Mother of God and of all Your Saints, grant me Your forgiveness and blessing. Through Christ Our Lord.   Amen.

(If a high or special Holy Day Incense may be used: *"May you be blessed in Whose honor, you are to be burnt"*)

* (After, pray the *theme* of the Mass of the Day corresponding
   with an appropriate Scriptural verse, or the Psalms especially,
   and concludes with a Glory Be To The Father… check the Mass
   Liturgical Calendar Appendix in the book for suggestions).

The Kyrie

Lord, Have Mercy   (God, the Father)
Christ, Have Mercy   (God, the Son)
Lord, Have Mercy   (God, The Holy Spirit)

16

in excelsis deo!

Next: Pray the Gloria with extended hands

(Omit this when purple or black vestments are used)

Glory To GOD In The Highest! And On Earth Peace,
Goodwill Toward Men.
We Praise You,
We Bless You,
We Adore You,
We Glorify You,
We Give You Thanks For Your Great Glory:
O' Lord God, Heavenly King,
God Almighty Father!
O' Lord JESUS CHRIST, The Only-Begotten Son;
O' Lord God, Lamb of God, Son of The Father:

17

Who Takes Away The Sins Of The World,
Have Mercy On Us;
You Who Takes Away The Sins Of The World,
Receive Our Prayer;
Who Sits At The Right Hand Of The Father,
Have Mercy On Us.
For You Alone Are Holy,
You Alone Are The LORD,
You Alone, O' Jesus Christ,

Are Most High,
Together With The HOLY SPIRIT
In The Glory Of God The Father.   *AMEN.*

Look up to Heaven and Say:

May the Lord be with us, let us all pray...
(After this, a prayer addressing the Solemnity, Feast,
or Memorial of the day. This will be found in the Appendix.)

Then conclude with this ending:
Through Jesus Christ, Your Son, Our Lord, Who lives
and reigns with You in the unity of the Holy Ghost, One
God forever and ever.   ***AMEN.***

18

Liturgy of the Word

The First Reading:

(Taken from the Mass of the Day, the reading is an instruction
derived from the Old Testament for weekdays, the Epistles on

Sundays, and on Eastertide and Holy Days, the Book of Acts).
Read quietly or sing the passage and conclude:

Thanks Be To God.

The Psalm

(After this, go to the Appendix of Day Readings and recite the
Psalm and its response appropriate to the occasion.)

The Gradual and The Alleluia

**(The Gradual is an affirmation drawn from Scripture and
formed as a comment on an important mystery of the
Faith. It is employed during Lent in place of the Alleluia.
In former times, the Tract, seen in older missals is taken
up by the Responsorial Psalm more appropriately. See the
Appendix for both, according to the day.)**

During Lent use one these acclamations after the gradual:

1) *Praise to You, Lord Jesus Christ, King of Endless Glory!*
2) *Praise and Honor to You, Lord Jesus Christ!*
3) *Glory and Praise to You, Lord Jesus Christ!*
4) *Glory to You, O' Word of God, Lord Jesus Christ!*

20

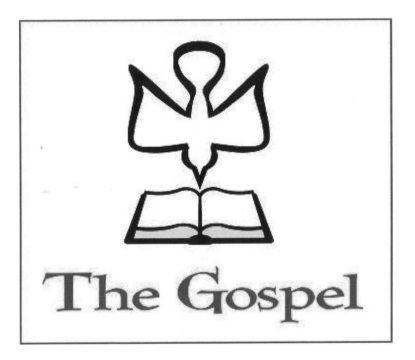

(Refer to the Mass of the Day and Season from the Appendix.
Incense the page on high holy days and solemnities).

With bowed head toward the altar,
the priest says the following prayer
in low tones:

*Cleanse my heart and lips O' God, as You cleansed
those of Your prophet Isaiah with a burning flame;
and in Your gracious mercy, purify me that I may
be made worthy to proclaim the words of Your Holy
Gospel fittingly and to Your Glory. Through Christ
Our Lord.   AMEN.*

Then take the Gospels and turn aside or away from the
altar and say:

21

A reading of the Holy Gospel according to...
(St. Matthew, St. Mark, St. Luke, or St. John, refer to the
indications from the Appendix in back for the day/season.
Trace the Sign of the Cross with the thumb on the forehead,

lips, and heart.)

Then say: ***Glory Be To You, O' Lord.***

Read, Recite, or Sing the Passage.

At the end of the Gospel say:

Praise to You Lord Jesus Christ

Kiss the sacred page and pray:

***By the words of this Holy Gospel may my sins
be blotted out.***

22

**Instructed, moved, and renewed by the Word of God, one
is prepared to consider how to respond to the Gospels through**

one's way of life. Next, we profess what we believe.

The Creed
Sabbath and Holy Days

The Nicene Creed:

We believe in one God,

The Father, The Almighty,

Maker of Heaven and Earth,

Of all things visible and invisible.

We believe in one Lord, Jesus Christ,

The only Son of God,

Eternally begotten of The Father,

God from God; Light from Light;

True God from true God,

Begotten, not made; consubstantial with The Father.

Through Him, all things were made.

For us men, and for our salvation

He came down from Heaven;   (Bow)

By the Power of The Holy Spirit

He was born of the Virgin Mary,

And became man.   **(Lift head again)**

For our sake He was crucified under Pontius Pilate;

He suffered, died, and was buried.

On the third day He rose again

In fulfillment of the Scriptures;

He ascended into Heaven

And is seated at the right Hand of The Father.

He will come again in glory to judge the living and the dead,

And his Kingdom will have no end.

We believe in The Holy Spirit, The Lord and Giver of Life,

Who proceeds from The Father and The Son.

With The Father and The Son, He is worshiped and glorified.

He has spoken through the Prophets.

We believe in one holy and apostolic Church.

We acknowledge one baptism for the forgiveness of sins.

We look for the resurrection of the dead,

And the life of the world to come.   *AMEN.*

Credo
for Weekdays

The Apostles Creed:

I believe in God, The Father Almighty,
Creator of Heaven and Earth.
I believe in Jesus Christ, His only Son, our Lord.
Who was conceived by the Power of The Holy Spirit
And born of the Virgin Mary.
He suffered under Pontius Pilate,
Was crucified, died, and was buried.
He descended into Hell.
On the third day He rose again.
He ascended into Heaven,
And is seated at the right hand of The Father.
He will come again to judge the living and the dead.
I believe in The Holy Spirit,
The holy Catholic Church,
The communion of saints, the forgiveness of sins,

The resurrection of the body, and life everlasting.   *AMEN.*

General Intercessions

Lord of all goodness, You instructed your faithful to ask of The Father anything in Your Name, and it shall be granted and so, I intercede for Your people:

(Here, mention each all the intentions and requests you received and those for the Church).

Lord, hear my prayer.   **AMEN.** (At the last)

Liturgy of the Holy Eucharist

Offertory Hymn   (Prayer is found in the Appendix).
Remove the linens from the Chalice and set on the right hand side. Take the Paten with the host upon it (or place it there), and hold it up at chest height.

27

Accept, O Holy Father, Almighty and Eternal God, this immaculate Host, which I, Your unworthy servant, offer to You, my true and Living God, for my own countless sins and weaknesses; for all here present, and all Thy faithful Christians, living and deceased, that it may become the means of salvation unto Eternal Life in Thy Kingdom for me and for them.   AMEN.

Pour the Wine into the Chalice at this time, then a
little Water (symbolizing the mingling of Jesus
divinity with the humanity of mankind).

Pray:

*O God, Who wonderfully created and exalted our human
nature and even more wondrously glorified it in Your Son
Jesus Christ; may we become partakers in His Divinity as
He was pleased to partake of our humanity. Who lives and
reigns with You in the unity of The Holy Spirit, One God,
forever and ever.*   *AMEN.*

Continue, taking the Chalice and raising it chest-high:

Lord, we offer You, this saving Chalice and beg of Your Mercy, that it may be as a sweet fragrance in the Majesty of Your Divine Presence for our salvation and that of our whole world.   *AMEN.*

Bow a little, and pray:

Come O' Holy Spirit, Almighty Sanctifier and Ever-Living God, and bless this sacrifice prepared for the glory of Your Holy Name.

On High Holy Days, Incense should be offered up with prayer:

May the Lord be pleased to bless this incense and to receive its sweet fragrance through the intercession of the Blessed Archangel Michael, who stands at the right hand of the altar of incense and of the Lord's chosen people. Through Christ our Lord.   AMEN.

OR

Let my prayer come up like incense before You, Lord; the lifting up of my hands, like the evening sacrifice.

OR

May the Lord enkindle in us the fire of His love and the flame of everlasting charity.   AMEN.

Incense the offerings in the form of a cross, then incense the Crucifix and the altar.

The Washing of the Hands

*As I go about Your altar O'Lord, let me give voice to
my thanks and praise of You for all Your wondrous deeds!
For I love to dwell in the House of Your Glory. Let not
my soul be gathered with the wicked, but wash away my
iniquities and in your mercy, cleanse me from my sins.*

Glory Be…. Etc...   (Omit Gloria at requiems).

31

Prayer to the Holy Trinity

Receive O' Most Holy Trinity, this sacrifice we make to you in commemoration of the Passion, Resurrection, and Ascension of our Lord Jesus Christ and in honor of the Blessed Mother of God, Mary ever-Virgin, Of Blessed Joseph, her spouse most chaste, Of the Blessed Apostles Peter and Paul and (the saints of the altar stone and/ or the day). *And of all the Saints that through our honor on earth they may be pleased to intercede for us in Heaven and be helpful to our salvation. Through the same Christ our Lord.*   *AMEN.*

May the Lord receive the sacrifice at my hands, to the praise and glory of His Name, for my good and for that of all His Holy Church.   *AMEN.*

32

The Eucharistic Prayers

May the Lord bless me as I raise my heart and hands to praise and glorify His lovingkindness. May all the Earth render Him thanks as is fitting, proper, and just to do.

Common Preface/ Secret Prayer

(Proper prefaces for the day may be found in the Appendix)

Indeed, it is truly right, most appropriate, proper and advantageous to our salvation that we should always and everywhere give you thanks Lord, Holy Father, Almighty and Eternal God through Jesus Christ our Lord. Through Whom, all the Angels praise Your holy Majesty. The Dominions worship You, the Powers gaze upon You in Awe. I join my voice with that of all Heaven and Its Hosts, with the Seraphim and Cherubim in humble exaltation unceasingly:
Holy, Holy, Holy, Lord God of Hosts! Heaven and Earth are full of Your Glory. Hosanna in the Highest! Blessed is He Who comes in the Name of The Lord. Hosanna in the Highest!

33

(Ring the bell three times in Thanksgiving)

1. Kiss the Altar

2. **Genuflect**

34

<u>Blessing of the Gifts</u>

Incline toward Altar

Therefore, most gracious Father, I humbly entreat You through Jesus Christ Your Son, our Lord,

Then over the gifts:

to deem acceptable, bless and, sanctify these unspotted oblations which we offer you firstly for Your Holy Catholic Church, to give her days of peace and protection throughout the world together with the Pope of Rome, and all bishops, priests, ministers and devoted servants who cherish the Faith we received from Your Apostles.

35

Commemoration of the Living

Remember, O'Lord Your children and servants here on earth (Name them), *whose faith and devotion are known to You, on whose behalf I offer this sacrifice of praise for them, their families, and friends, for the good of their souls, their hope of salvation, and deliverance from all evil, who come to pay homage to You, the One True, Eternal, and Ever-Living God.*

Communicantes of the Feastday

("Being in Fellowship and keeping..." Announce the prayer of the observance of the Day from the Appendix)

Commemoration of the Saints

In communion with the holy fellowship of of the Saints, we observe the memory firstly of Your glorious and immaculate Mother, Mary Ever-Virgin, and of the Blessed Joseph, her most-chaste spouse, of St. Michael and of all Your holy angels and archangels, of your blessed Patriarchs, Prophets, and Martyrs: Peter and Paul, Andrew, James and John, Thomas, James the brother of the Lord, Philip, Bartholomew, Matthew, Simon and Jude; of Stephen Linus, Cletus, Clement, Mary of Magdala, Agatha, Lucy, Agnes, Cecilia, Felicity and Perpetua ... and with all your Saints who have sought and done Your will throughout the centuries. Admit us to their company, not considering what we deserve, but granting us Your free and rich pardon.   *AMEN.*

37

Bless the Offerings

(Five times make the Sign of the Cross)

O' GOD deign to bless   what we offer, and make it

approved,   effective,   right and favorable in

every way, that it may become for our good The Body

and Blood   *of Your dearly beloved Son our Lord,*
Jesus Christ.

<u>**(Bow to effect the Consecration)**</u>

<u>*The Transubstantiation:*</u>

CONSECRATION OF THE HOST

Who, the evening before He suffered, took bread into His holy and venerable hands, and having raised His eyes to You, our Almighty Father in Heaven, gave thanks,

✠

blessed it,   broke it, and gave it to His disciples saying: Take This All of You and Eat of It:

FOR THIS IS MY BODY WHICH IS BROKEN FOR YOU, DO THIS IN MEMORY OF ME.

(Say devoutly, secretly: *MY LORD, AND MY GOD!***)**

Ring bell thrice in thanks:

Then genuflect:

CONSECRATION OF THE WINE

(Again leaning close into the Altar)

In like manner, when supper was ended, taking also the holy cup into His sacred and venerable hands, and giving special thanks

✠

Holy Father, He blessed it   *and gave it to His disciples saying: All of you take, and drink of this:*

For This Is The Chalice of My Blood of the New and Eternal Covenant:

40

Which is Shed For You and For Many, For The Forgiveness of Sins. This Do, in Remembrance of Me.

(My Lord and My God!)

Thus, we commemorate O' Lord our GOD, not only the blessed Passion and Death of Your Son Our Lord Jesus Christ, but moreover, of His triumphant Resurrection

and glorious Ascension into Heaven. In this spirit, I

Your minister, of the gifts you have granted to us, offer to You this pure and spotless Victim, the bread of Eternal Life, and the Chalice of unending Salvation. Look upon my action with gracious and kindly acceptance, as You once did with that of Your servant Abel, and the sacrifice of Abraham our father in faith, and of Melchizedek, Your first Holy Chief Priest. May our offering be borne up by the hands of Your Holy Angel to Your altar above in the Presence of Your Divine Majesty, That I am all those who partake of the Body and Blood of Your Son may be filled with every grace and blessing of Heaven. Through Christ our Lord. **AMEN.**

<u>Commemoration of The Dead</u>

Remember also, Our Lord, we appeal to Thee, Your children (N.N) who have gone on before us in the sleep of peace under the sign of Faith. To these grant a place of comfort, light, and eternal happiness with Your holy Angels and Saints. Through Christ our Lord. **AMEN.**

For Whom, O' Loving GOD, You always create, in Whom You Sanctify, and by Whom You fill with Life, bless bestow upon us all good things.

<u>The Minor Elevation and Presentation</u>

(Hold the Host and Chalice up as shown above)

Through Him, with Him, and in Him. In the unity of the Holy Spirit, is all glory and Honor to You Almighty Father, forever and ever, world without end.   AMEN.

(Another posture to use)

43

(Genuflect)

Communion and Thanksgiving

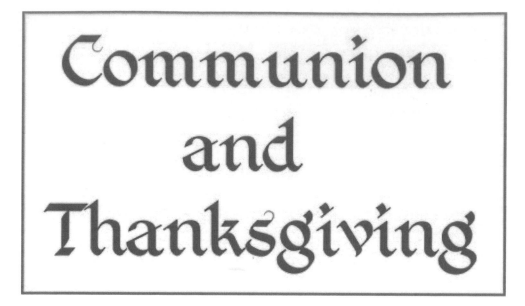

Prompted by Your saving precepts and guided by
Your Divine Inspiration, I dare to say:

Our Father, Who art in Heaven, hallowed be Thy Name. Thy kingdom come, Thy will be done, on Earth as it is in Heaven. Give us this day, our daily bread, and forgive us our trespasses as we forgive those who trespass against us. And lead us not into temptation, but deliver us from evil. AMEN.

44

Deliver us Lord, I pray from every evil, past, present and those to come and by the intercession of the blessed and glorious Virgin Mary, and all the court of angels and saints, grant us Your goodness, peace in our time, and through Your Mercy preserve us from disturbance and terror. AMEN.

The Fraction:

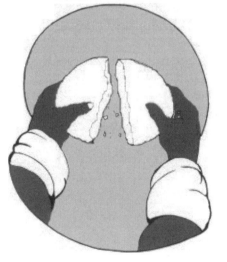

(Over the chalice, break the host in two, then break a small chip off and drop it into the chalice saying:)

May the mingling of the Body and Blood of our Lord Jesus Christ help those of us who receive it to attain life everlasting in God. AMEN.

45

The Agnus Dei

*LAMB OF GOD, Who take away the sins of the World,
have mercy on us.*
*LAMB OF GOD, Who take away the sins of the World,
have mercy on us.*
*LAMB OF GOD, Who take away the sins of the World,
grant us peace.*

(At this juncture, pronounce the commemorative prayer
and communion hymn found in the Appendix of the day)

Prayers Before Communion

For Unity and Peace:

My Lord Jesus Christ, Who said to Your Apostles: "Peace I leave with you, My peace, I give to you", do not consider my sins, but upon my faith in You and Your Holy Church, and I pray that You grant her peace and unity according to Your Will: Who live and reign, God, world without end.   AMEN.

For Holiness:

Jesus, Son of the Living God, and Promise of Ages, at The Father's Will, and in the strength of The Holy Spirit, Your death has extended the life of the world. Save me by this Your most precious Body and Blood, from all my sins and from every evil. Cause me to hold fast to Your commandments and never permit me to fall away from You, Who live and reign with God the Father and The Holy Spirit, world without end.   AMEN.

For Worthiness:

Let not my presumption to take Your Body and Blood, O' Lord Jesus my Savior, incur Your righteous reproach and condemnation against me, though most unworthy, but through Your goodness, may it become an effective

remedy and powerful safeguard of both my soul and body. Who live and reign with God the Father in the Unity of The Holy Spirit, Forever and Ever.   AMEN.

I will take the Bread of Heaven, calling upon the Name of The LORD.

(Recite the following prayer 3x, ringing the bell each time.)

(LORD, I am not worthy that you should come under my roof, but only say the Word, and my soul shall be healed.) May the Body of Christ preserve my soul to life everlasting. AMEN.

Act of Hope

What return shall I make to Thee O' my Lord Jesus for all Thou hast given me? I will take Your Chalice of Salvation calling upon Your Most Holy Name in praise and thanksgiving. Thus, I shall be saved from my enemies.

May the Blood of Christ preserve my soul to life everlasting. AMEN.

What has passed my lips as food O' Lord, may I retain in purity of heart, that what has been partaken in time, heal me unto Eternity. May Your Body Lord, which I have eaten, and Your Blood, which I have drunk, cleave to my very soul, and grant that no trace of sin be found within me, to whom these pure, and holy mysteries have been renewed. Who live and reign world without end.   *AMEN.*

May this tribute of my worship be pleasing and acceptable to You O' Most Holy Trinity, and grant that this sacrifice which I, wholly unworthy, have offered in the Presence of Your Majesty may obtain Your mercy and pardon for me and for all whom I have offered it. In the Most Holy Name of Jesus, Our Lord.   *AMEN.*

May your servant withdraw in Your Peace and Blessing.

49

(At this point, if time permits, it is beneficial to recite five decades of the Rosary, and the Hail Holy Queen; Appendix)

And then this Prayer:

O' GOD our refuge and strength, look down with mercy on Your people who cry out unto You; and by the intercession of the glorious and Immaculate Virgin Mary, the Mother of God, of Saint Joseph, her most chaste spouse, Of Your Blessed Apostles especially Peter and Paul, and of all the Saints and Angels, kindly hear our prayers for the conversion of us sinners and the triumph of Your Holy Church. Through the same Christ Jesus, Our Lord.   AMEN.

(Prayer of St. Michael the Archangel; Index)

Three times:
Most Sacred Heart of Jesus, Have Mercy on Us.

Sign of the Cross:

End of the private Rite of the Roman Mass.

50

✝ The Holy Mass ✝

Extracted from Novus Ordo Missae

A very good liturgy for Sundays and regular days in ordinary time (but not Lent, Easter, Advent or solemnities).

(All Stand)

(Entrance Antiphon (Taken from the Appendix for the day lead by the priest and taken up by the people).

The priest then processes toward the altar alone if no other assistants are present. The altar is set, the priest merely carries his veiled chalice to the altar.

Either alone or with assistants, reverence the Altar by genuflection or bow:

Then turn round clockwise and face the people:

Priest and All say:

In the Name of the Father and of the Son and the Holy Spirit.   *AMEN.*

Stand in front of the Altar facing the people and greet them saying:

52

Priest: *"The peace of Our Lord Jesus Christ, the Grace of God, and the Love of the Holy Spirit be with you all".*

People: "And with your spirit".

Opening Prayer from Appendix)

At this point of the service, the priest may briefly introduce the Mass-of-the-day (saying something about the readings, the feast or solemnity, or the intentions of the celebration).

This being done, he may proceed with a short but traditional purification blessing, as is his option. In ancient times no one entered the Temple without ritual immersion. The use of holy water stands in place of this today.

53

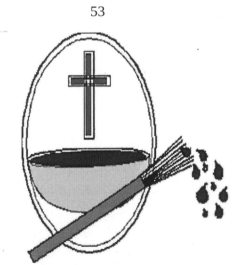

The Blessing Rite and the Sprinkling of Holy Water

Priest:

"Dear Friends, this water will be used to remind us of our baptism. Let us ask God to bless it, and to keep us faithful to the Spirit He has

given us."

(Make the sign of the Cross over the water and pray)
"Lord God Almighty, Creator of all life, body, and soul, we ask You to bless this water: as we use it in faith, forgive us our sins, and save us from all sickness and the power of evil.

Lord, in Your Mercy, give us living water, always springing up as a fountain of salvation: free us body and soul from every danger, and admit us to Your presence in purity of heart.

We ask this through Christ our Lord".   **ALL: AMEN.**

54

While sprinkling, pray:

"May Almighty God cleanse us from our sins, and through the Holy Eucharist we celebrate, make us worthy to sit at His table in the Kingdom of Heaven."

ALL: AMEN.

(This rite is used at Eastertide, Solemnities, and Feastdays. Do not use it during Lent or funerals. On ordinary days or Memorials of Saints, you may use the Penitential Rite).

The Penitential Rite

"As we prepare to celebrate the mystery of
Christ's love, let us acknowledge our
failures and ask the Lord for pardon and strength."

55

(After a period of silence)

Priest & People:

"I confess to Almighty God, and to you my
brothers and sisters, that I have sinned through
my own fault, in my thoughts and in my words,
in what I have done, and in what I have failed
to do; And I ask Blessed Mary, ever Virgin, all
the angels and saints, and you, my brothers and
sisters, to pray for me to the Lord our God."

"May Almighty God have mercy on us,

Priest   *forgive us our sins, and bring us to*

everlasting life."

ALL: **"AMEN."**

" LORD, HAVE MERCY"

"LORD, Have Mercy"

"CHRIST, HAVE MERCY"

" CHRIST, Have Mercy"

"LORD, HAVE MERCY"

"LORD, Have Mercy"

The Gloria (omitted Lent/Advent)

"Let us offer praise to God in Heaven after the manner of His Angels"

"Glory to God in the Highest,
and peace to His People on Earth.
Lord God, Heavenly King, Almighty God
and Father, we worship You, we give You
thanks, we praise You for Your Glory.
Lord Jesus Christ, only Son of the Father,
Lord God, Lamb of God, You take away

the sin of the world: *have mercy on us;*
You are seated at the Right Hand of the
Father: *receive our prayer.*

58

For You alone are the Holy One, You alone
are the Lord, You alone are the Most High,
Jesus Christ, with the Holy Spirit, in the
Glory of God the Father."   AMEN.

The Gradual

This is to be taken from the Mass of the

Day (Theme, Feast, or Memorial) found

in the Appendix.)

The people then say: **AMEN.**

(All Sit)

Lector: " A reading from the Book of..."

(O.T. Prophets, Epistle, or Acts).

At the conclusion:

Lector: *"The Word of the Lord"*

People: **"Thanks be to God"**

60

The Responsorial Psalm

This will be taken from the Psalms in which the Lector will recite, and the people will respond with a Psalm. Proverbs and Ecclesiastes can also be used. This is in the Lectionary of the Season. This may also be choral.

The Alleluia / Gospel Acclamation

Priest or Cantor: **"Alleluia!"**

(All Stand)   **The People:**   **"Alleluia!"**

The Priest or Cantor acclaims the appropriate **verse** from the Lectionary

and ends, **"Alleluia, Alleluia"**

The People: **"Alleluia!"**

The preceding rite is altered according to season:

"Alleluia": to be spoken Easter – Ordinary Time twice or more.

" Praise to You Lord Jesus Christ" for Lent.

For Advent: Priest: "Indeed I am coming soon"

People: "Even so, Come Lord Jesus"

Priest: "A reading from the Holy Gospel
According to...(any four Evangelists by season)

(Priest and people make three small cross signs
forehead, lips, and heart)

People: "Glory to You, Lord!"

After the Gospel Reading:

Priest: "The Gospel of the Lord."

People: "Praise to You Lord Jesus Christ!"

63

(All Sit)

The Homily

The Homily is basically a "Fireside Chat" from earliest times and invited questions and responses for the edification of the Faith. Sermons are more formal and lack this (probably due to numbers of people). Jesus spoke in homily, as did many philosophers of the time.

The priest performs this now, or with his blessing invites another to speak an important message.

The Profession of Faith

All are to recite these, Priest and Congregants. The first is the oldest statement of belief, created by the Apostles. The second, the Creed composed at the Imperial Church Council of Nicaea in 325 AD.   **(All Stand)**

Priest: *"Let us now profess what we believe."*

The Apostle's Creed

"I believe in God, The Father Almighty...

65

"The Maker of Heaven and Earth,

And in Jesus Christ, His only Son, Our Lord.

Who was conceived by the power of the Holy Spirit,

and born of the Virgin Mary. He suffered under Pontius

Pilate, was crucified, died and was buried.

He descended into Hell.

On the third day He rose again.

He ascended into Heaven, and is seated at the right

hand of the Father.

He will come again to judge the Living and the Dead.

I believe in the Holy Spirit, the Holy Catholic Church,
the Communion of Saints, the forgiveness of sins,
the resurrection of the body, and life everlasting.
AMEN.

The following is the Creed of Nicaea used on Sundays and High
Holy Days:

<u>The Nicene Creed</u>

We believe in one God, the Father, The Almighty,
The Maker of Heaven and Earth, of all that is seen and unseen.
We believe in one Lord Jesus Christ, the only Son of God,

66

eternally begotten of the Father, God from God,
Light, from Light, true God from true God.
Begotten, not made, one in being with the Father.
Through Him, all things were made.
For us men, and for our salvation, He came down from Heaven
(Bow the head for the next two lines)
By the power of the Holy Spirit, He was born of the Virgin Mary,
and became man.
For our sake He was crucified under Pontius Pilate;
He suffered, died, and was buried. On the third day He rose again
in fulfillment of the scriptures; He ascended into Heaven, and is
seated at the right hand of the Father. He will come again in glory
to judge the living and the dead, and His kingdom will have no end.
We believe in the Holy Spirit; the Lord and Giver of Life,
Who proceeds from the Father and the Son.

With the Father and the Son, He is worshiped and glorified.

He has spoken through the Prophets.

We believe in one holy Catholic and Apostolic Church.

We acknowledge one baptism for the forgiveness of sins.

We look for the resurrection of the dead, and the life of

the world to come.   Amen.

67

(Priest, but ideally a Deacon, Lector, or Cantor)

"Let us now submit our requests to God and intercede for others"

(At the end of each petition, the leader intones)

"Let us pray to the Lord"

People: **"Lord Hear Our Prayer"**

(All Sit)

(Customary time for

Collection or Song)

Liturgy
of the
Eucharist

The Offertory Prayer:

(The Priest may step to the front or right front side of Altar to say this appropriate All-Occasion Offertory prayer or intone one from the Appendix for the Mass of the Day.)

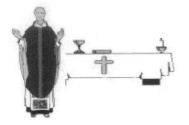

or

69

Priest: *"Heavenly Father, we offer You these gifts to mend the hearts of those who are in the thrall of the Evil One. You alone have the power to remove our iniquities; our avarice, our prejudices, and our fears.*
Your word alone can nurture our souls and bring peace to our hearts. You have given us the gift of Salvation and You ask nothing save our repentance in return.
Your example of generosity teaches us to do the same especially those who have sinned against us.
You have taught us the lesson of forgiveness and so, we dedicate these gifts to Your Honor and Glory in thanksgiving for all the things You have given us and to commit ourselves and trust only in You all the days of our lives. We therefore dedicate our lives, hard work and sacrifices to You, Father, in Jesus Name, we pray.

(Priest and People)   *AMEN.*

(Return attention to the Altar. Remove the linens from the
chalice and place to the right. Take the Paten with the
Host upon it and raise it chest-height.)

70

Priest Says: *"Blessed are You, Lord God of all creation.*
Through Your goodness we have this bread

*to offer, which earth has given and human
hands have made. It will become for us, the*

Bread of Life."

Sign of the Cross, with Paten, sliding *Host upon Corporal*.)

People Say: "Blessed be God forever".

(The Priest then takes the Chalice, pouring wine then a little water)

Priest: *"By the Mystery of this water
and wine, may we come to share
in the Divinity of Christ, Who
humbled Himself to share in our
humanity."*

71

(After pouring, raise the chalice chest high)

Priest Says: *"Blessed are You, Lord God of all creation,*
Through Your goodness, we have this wine
to offer, fruit of the vine, and work of
human hands. It will be come for us our

spiritual drink."

(Place on Corporal)

People exclaim: "Blessed be God Forever!"

(Priest quietly prays the following prayer and bows. After this
the Gifts, Altar, and People are incensed if Solemn High Mass).

*"With humble and contrite heart, may we be accepted by You,
O'Lord, and may our sacrifice in Your sight this day be pleasing
to You, Lord God."*

(Turning to the right side, a table preferably, the priest pours
water on his hands and dries them. Deacon/acolyte can aid)

Priest: *"Lord, wash away my iniquity,
cleanse me from my sins."*

(Priest adopts the Orant position of arms outstretched)

(Stand)

Priest: *"Pray my brothers and sisters, that our sacrifice*
may be acceptable to God, the Almighty Father."

People: **"May The Lord accept the sacrifice**
at your hands, for the praise and glory
of His Name, for our good, and the good
of all His Church."

73

the transubstantiation

Priest: *"The Lord be with you!"*

(If a Bishop) "Peace be with You!"

People: "And with your spirit!"

Priest: (Lifting hands a little higher and the people also.)

"Lift up your hearts!"

74

People: "We lift them up to the Lord."

Priest: *"Let us give thanks to the Lord our God!"*

People: "It is right and just."

(Now follows the Preface /Secret Prayer before Holy Transubstantiation and Communion. Seasonal and Solemn prayers for the Holydays and observances may be found in the Appendix. These two are presented as traditional and beautiful forms of this invocation.)

(Adopt this posture)

75

Eucharistic Prayer I

"Father, it is our duty, and our salvation, always and everywhere to give You thanks through Your beloved Son, our Lord, Jesus Christ.
He is the word through whom You made all Creation, the Savior You sent to redeem us. By the power of the Holy Spirit, He took flesh and was born of the Virgin Mary.
For our sake, He opened His arms on the cross, He put an end to death, and revealed the Resurrection. In this, He fulfilled Your will, and won for You a Holy people.

And so, we join the angels and saints in proclaiming Your glory…" (Then the Sanctus).

Eucharistic Prayer II

Our Father in Heaven, it is only right that we should give You thanks and glory: You are the One True and Living God. At the heart of Eternity, You dwell in unapproachable Light.
Source of all life and goodness, You have created all

things, to fill Your creatures with every blessing and lead all to the joyful vision of Your radiance. The Angelic hosts beyond counting, stand before You to perform Your Will; they behold Your Glory and praise You unceasingly.
United with them, and in the name is every creature under Heaven, we too praise Your glory, as we say:

The Sanctus

Priest & People: *"Holy, Holy Holy, **Lord** God **of Power** and **Might!** Heaven **and Earth** are full **of** Your Glory! **Hosanna, in the** Highest! **Blessed** is He Who **comes** in **the** Name **of** the **Lord.** Hosanna **in the Highest!"***

(People Kneel)

Posture for the Epiclesis
(Calling upon the Holy Spirit)

Priest: *"Father, we acknowledge Your greatness; all Your actions show Your wisdom and love. You formed humanity in Your own image, and set us over the entire world to serve You, our Maker, and to take governance over all other creatures. Even when we disobeyed and lost Your friendship, You did not abandon us to the power of death, but helped all Your children to seek and find You. Time after time, You offered a covenant to us and through the Prophets, taught us to hope for Salvation.*

Father, You so loved the World, that in the fullness of time, You sent Your only Son to be our Savior. He was conceived through the power of the Holy Spirit, and born of the Virgin, Mary. A man like us in all ways, but sin. To the poor He proclaimed the good news of Salvation. To prisoners, freedom, to those in sorrow, joy. In fulfillment of Your will, He gave Himself up to the power of Death, but rising from the dead, destroyed death, and restored Life. And that we might live no longer for ourselves, but for Him, He sent the Holy Spirit, from You Father, as His first gift to those who believe, to carry on His work and bring us to the fullness of grace.

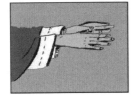

✠   *Father, may this same Holy Spirit, sanctify these*

offerings. Let them become the Body
(make sign of the cross) *and Blood of Jesus Christ, Our Lord as we celebrate the great mystery which he left us as an everlasting covenant."*

Shorter Version:

"Lord, You are Holy indeed, the fountain of all holiness.

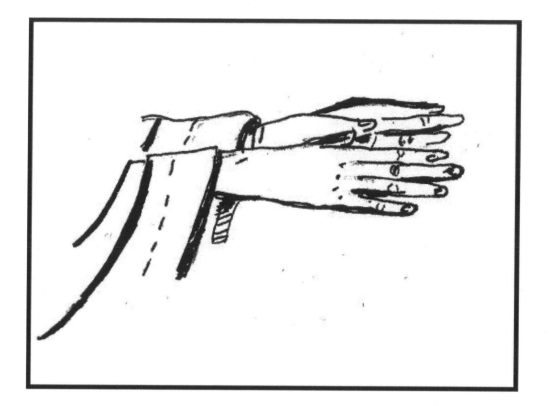

Let Your Spirit come upon these gifts to make them

holy, so they may become the Body

And Blood of Our Lord, Jesus Christ."

(Ring bell in thanks)

"Before He was given up to death, a death He freely
accepted. He took bread in His sacred hands, and
blessing it, gave You Father, thanks and praise.
He broke the bread, gave it to His disciples and said:

"Take This All of You and Eat it. This is My Body Which Will Be Given Up For You"

80

(Raise High the Host)

(Ring Thrice)

(Place the consecrated Host On the *Corporal, not on Paten*)

(Genuflect/ or bow low)

(Then, taking the Chalice, and raising it mid-height he says:)

Priest: *"When supper was ended, He took the cup, again*
           He gave You thanks and praise, gave the cup to
           His disciples and said,"

81

"Take This All of You, and Drink From It. This Is The Cup of My Blood. The Blood Of The New and Everlasting Covenant. It Will Be Shed For You and For Many For The Forgiveness of Sins. Do This In Memory of Me."

(Raise the Chalice High for a few moments and set on Corporal)

(Ring Thrice)

82

(Genuflect/ or Low Bow again)

Priest: "Let us proclaim the Mystery of Faith"

Priest & People **say one of the following:**

A) "Christ **has Died, Christ is Risen,** Christ **will come Again.**"

B) "**Dying** You **destroyed** our **death,** Rising, **Your** restored **our** Life, **Lord** Jesus **come** in **Glory.**"

C) "When we Eat **this Bread, and** Drink **this Cup, we** proclaim **Your** death Lord Jesus, **Until** You **come** in **Glory.**"

D) "Lord, **by** Your **Cross** and **Resurrection,** You **have** set Us free, **You** are **the** Savior **of the World.**"

The Anamnesis, Offerings, and Intercessions

Priest:

"Father, we celebrate the memory of Christ, Your Son.
We, Your people and ministers, recall His Passion, His
Resurrection from the dead, and His Ascension into Glory;
and from the many gifts You have given us we offer to You,
God of glory and majesty, this holy and perfect sacrifice:
The Bread of Life and The Cup of Eternal Salvation.

Look with favor upon these offerings as You once accepted
the gift of Your servant Abel, the sacrifice of Abraham, our
father in faith, and the bread and wine offered by Your
priest Melchizedek."

"Almighty God, we pray that Your angel may take this
Sacrifice to place upon Your Most Holy Table in Heaven.
So that, as we receive the Sacred Body and Blood of
Your Son, from this altar on earth, we may be filled with
every grace and blessing. Through Christ Our Lord. Amen.

"Lord, remember those from whom we offer this Sacrifice.
Especially we mention Your Chief Vicar the Bishop of Rome,
and the fellowship of all Your bishops, priests, ministers,
and all men and women consecrated to the service of Your
Son's labors to save the Souls You have created. Remember
Your people, their chosen leaders, and all those present,
who seek You with a sincere heart.

Remember O' Lord our dearly departed who have gone
ahead of us on their journey to Your kingdom, for whom
we now pray; (Pronounce the names of the Deceased).
May these and all the Dead, whose faith and worthiness
is known to You alone, find Light, Happiness, and Peace
in the Kingdom of Your Son, Jesus Christ our Lord.
For ourselves, we too ask some share of the inheritance
and Heavenly fellowship You have bestowed upon Your
Saints and the Elect, who have served You down through

the ages unto this day. Make us worthy to share eternal
Life, with the Blessed Virgin Mary, the Mother of God,
and with her spouse, Joseph, foster father of our Redeemer,
St. John the Baptist, His august prophet; the holy Apostles

Peter and Paul, John and James, Andrew, Jude, Thomas, Bartholomew, James the son of Alpheus, Philip, Matthew, Simon, and Matthias.

May we enter into Your joy with Your holy Patriarchs and Prophets, Abraham, Moses, Elijah, and Daniel, and enjoy the company of Your blessed Martyrs and Confessors, Mark, Luke, Barnabas, Mary Magdalene, Lazarus, Timothy, Agnes, Agatha, Linus, Gregory (Name those of your relics, and church, and some modern saints in timely manner, and the saints of the day). *In the escort of Michael and all Your Holy Angels. Though we are sinners, we trust in Your mercy and love. Do not consider what we truly deserve, but grant us Your forgiveness. Through Christ our Lord.*

"AMEN"

"Then, in the splendor of Your Kingdom, forever freed from the corruption of sin and death, we shall sing Your Glory with every creature through Christ our Lord, through Whom, You have given us every grace and good."

(Replace Host on Paten by carefully sliding it, take Chalice in left lifting them chest-high).

Priest: *"Through Him, With Him, In Him, in the unity of the Holy Spirit, all glory and honor are Yours, Almighty Father, forever and ever."*

ALL: **"AMEN!"**

(The Great Amen may be said 3 times or best, sung)

<u>Rite of Holy Communion</u>
The Lord's Prayer

(The priest-celebrant will begin by announcing
any one of the following prefaces)

Priest: A) *"Our Savior commanded us to pray always*
as He received from His Father, and so we pray..."

B) *"Let us pray for the coming of The Kingdom*
as Jesus taught us."

C) *"Let us pray with confidence to the Father in*
the words, our Savior gave us."

D) *"Let us ask our Father to forgive our sins, and*
to bring us to forgive those who sin against us."

88

"Our Father, which art in Heaven, hallowed be Thy Name.

Thy Kingdom come, Thy Will be done, in Earth, as it is in

Heaven. Give us this day, our daily bread, and forgive us

our debts, as we forgive our debtors. Lead us not into temptation, but deliver us from evil."

"Deliver us Lord, from every evil, and grant us

peace to live out or lifetimes. In Your Mercy,

keep us free from sin, and protect us from

fear and worry, while we await in hope and

faith, the return of our Savior, Jesus Christ."

All:

"For the Kingdom, and the Power, and the

Glory are Yours, now and forever. AMEN."

89

The Sign of Peace

Priest: *"Lord Jesus Christ, You said to your Apostles, I leave you peace, My Peace, I give*
to you. Look not on our sins, but on the faith of
Your Church, and grant us the peace and unity
of Your Kingdom, where You live forever and ever."

People: **"Amen."**

Priest: *"The peace of the Lord be with you*
always."

People: *"And with your spirit."*

Priest (*or Deacon*): *"Let us offer one another a sign of peace."*

90

AGNUS DEI

After the Priest-Celebrant makes a sign of peace to his
fellow priest/deacon/acolyte/assistant he proceeds back

**To the Altar, and, taking the Consecrated Host, he
Breaks it, and then _Breaks off a small piece and
drops it into the Chalice_. This can be done _over_
the Paten or the Chalice.**

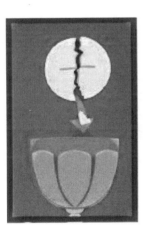

Like so…

Swirling the liquid VERY carefully, the Priest intones:

Priest: *"May the mingling of this Body and*
Blood of our Lord Jesus Christ bring
eternal life to us who receive it."

<u>The People:</u> (The People's Priesthood)
"LAMB of GOD, You take away the sins of the
World; Have mercy on US."
"LAMB of GOD, You take away the sins of the
World; Have mercy on US."
"LAMB of GOD, You take away the sins of the
World; Grant Us PEACE."

(The People Kneel)

92

While the people are praying the Agnus Dei, the priest,
bowed slightly toward the Altar, prays:

"Lord Jesus Christ, Son of the Living God,
Who, by the Will of the Father,
And the Work of the Holy Spirit,
Through Your Death provided Life to the World,
Free me by this, Your Most Holy Body and Blood,
From all my sins and from every evil;
Keep me always faithful to Your commandments,
And never let me be parted from You. AMEN.

(The Priest then Genuflects)

93

Rising and taking the host and Chalice like so,
presents to the people saying:

"Behold The LAMB of GOD.
Behold Him Who takes away the sins of
the World! Happy are those whom He calls
to His Supper." (May also cross the host pieces)

People and **Priest**

"**Lord, I am not worthy that YOU should enter under my roof,
But only say the Word, and my soul shall be healed.**"

94

The Priest then prays in a low voice:

*"May the Body of Christ preserve me unto
Life Eternal."* (Consume the Host).

*"May the Blood of Christ preserve me
unto Life Eternal."* (Drink all the Chalice).

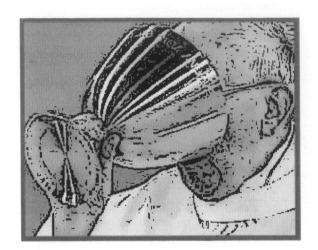

People: Intone the communion prayer
for the Mass of the day.

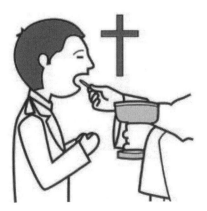

or

Priest: *"The Body of Christ."*

Person: "Amen."

Hymn Sing

There must be an assistant usually for the congregation to receive under both *species* (Host &Wine).

Next, the priest proceeds the Altar and starts the process of purifying the vessels.

97

Priest says this prayer as he is cleaning the vessels:

"What has passed our lips as food O'Lord,
may we possess in purity of heart
that what has been given to us in Time,
may be our healing in Eternity."

Do as follows: 1.

Pour water into the Chalice.
Swirl it around inside a bit.

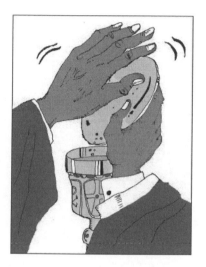

2. **Brush with the**
   thumb particles
   into the chalice.

3.

Drink the remaining

4.

Wipe dry with the Purificator

5. **Tri-fold the Purificator and place on the Chalice.**

6. **Take the Paten and place it atop the Purificator.**

7. **Place the Pall atop the Paten.**

Wash fingers in Ablution Cup.

98

The Priest may now sit down for a few
moments of reflection, even after song.

<u>Rites of Dismissal</u>

Special messages/announcements are now made.

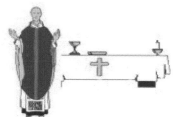

Priest: *"The Lord be with You"*

People: "And with your spirit."

Priest (Formal):

"Bow your heads and pray for God's Blessing"

(Priest will say a special blessing of occasion

which may come from the appendix).

Priest: *"May Almighty God bless you, In the Name of The Father, The Son, and The Holy Spirit."*

For a Bishop 3x , Once for each person of the Holy Trinity

Priest: *"The Mass is ended, go in peace;*

glorifying the Lord, by your life."

People: "Thanks be to God"
(Recessional Hymn)

100

These are listed as the useful and suggested format
of the traditional prayers spoken in the course of
the Mass according to the Solemn remembrance
or commemorative Feast Day. Priests may compose

their own prayers also.

Christmas Day
Introit/Antiphon:
"A Child is born unto us, and a Son is

> *given to us, Whose government shall*
> *be upon His shoulder; and His Name*
> *shall be called the Angel of Great*
> *Counsel."*

Collect (Called such because the Priest "collects" the prayers
of the faithful gathered and offers them up)
"Grant us, we pray, Almighty God, that Your only Son's
new Birth in the flesh may free us from our ancient slavery
to the bondage of sin. Through the same Christ our Lord."

101

The Gradual: *"Yours is Princely power in the day of*
  Your birth, in holy splendor, before the daystar, I
  have begotten You."
The Offertory: *"Yours and the heavens and Yours is*
  the Earth; the World and it's fullness You have founded;
  justice and judgment are the foundation of Your throne."
Secret Prayer: *"O' Lord may our offerings be worthy*

of the sacred rites of Your Nativity, and ever fill our hearts with peace. Christ, Who was born on this day as man, was also God; may our gift, which is of Earth, bestow upon us that which is divine. Through the same Jesus Christ, our Lord."

The People's Communion Prayer: *"Rejoice exceedingly O'Daughters of Zion, shout it abroad, O' Daughters of Jerusalem! For behold, Your King , the Holy One and Savior of the World has come."*

Post Communion Prayer: *"O' Lord, let us have new life through this ever-renewed sacramental coming of Christ, for by His birth as a child, He overcame the old sinful nature of mankind. Through the same Christ our Lord.*

Dismissal Benediction: *"May the Gift of God in His Son Jesus Christ our Lord, ever fill your hearts and souls on this Holy Day with peace and joy unto time everlasting."*

102

ADVENT

Advent Sunday/ Introit/Antiphon:
"I lift up my soul to You O' my God;
in You I place my trust. Let me not
be put to shame, nor let my enemies
gloat over me. No one who waits for
You shall be confounded.---

*"Make Your ways known to me O' Lord
and teach me Your paths...Glory be to
the Father, the Son, and the Holy Spirit,
as it was in the beginning, is now and ever
shall be, world without end.   AMEN."*

The Collect:

*"O' Lord, come to us in Your power and
might! Rescue us from the dangers that
threaten us because of our sins, and be
our salvation; Who lives and rules with
God the Father, in the unity of the Holy
Spirit, One God, forever and ever. AMEN."*

The Gradual:

*"No one who waits for You shall be left in
confusion. Make Your ways known to me
O' Lord and teach me Your paths."*

103

The Offertory:

*"I have lifted up my soul to You, O' my God;
in You I place my trust. Let me not be an
object of scorn, nor let those who hate me
ridicule me. No one who waits for You shall
ever be in confusion."*

Secret Prayer:

*"Let these sacred rites we perform cleanse
and purify us, O' Lord, that may bring us
closer to God, Who is their author. Through
our Lord."*

The People's Communion Prayer:
"The Lord will bestow His blessings,
 and the Earth shall yield up its fruits."
Post Communion Prayer:
"O' Lord, be merciful toward us kneeling
 before Your altar, so that we may prepare
 ourselves for a worthy celebration of the
 coming feast of our Redemption. Through
 Christ our Lord."
Dismissal: *"May the Spirit of God guide*
you as His Star arose and led all persons
in great joy to His revelation at Bethlehem."

Lenten Sunday
Entrance/Antiphon:
He shall call upon Me, and I will answer
him, I will deliver him and glorify him;
I will satisfy him with the fullness of life.
Glory be to the Father, and to the Son
 and to the Holy Spirit...   AMEN."
The Collect: *"O' Lord Who for our sake fasted for*

forty days and nights; strengthen us with the resolve
of such abstinence, that with our bodies thus
subdued, we may ever be open to the sublime stirrings
of Your Spirit, and follow You in the way of purity
and holiness to Calvary, and witness your glorious
triumph over death and the world."

<u>**The Gradual:**</u> *"Out of the depths, I cry unto*
You O' Lord! Lord, hear my voice! Let Your
ears be attentive to the prayer of Your servant.
If You O' Lord, count all of our sins, who can
stand? But with You, there is merciful forgiveness,
and because of Your law, I await You."

<u>**The Tract:**</u> (Used in place of the Alleluia, which
is not said again until Easter)

105

"O' Lord, repay us not according to the sins we
have committed, nor according to our iniquities.
O' Lord, remember not the offenses of our past;
but let Your Mercy come quickly to us, for we
have fallen far. (All Kneel)
"Help us O' God, our Savior, and for the glory
of Your Name O' Lord, deliver us; and pardon
our sins for Your name's sake."

<u>**The Offertory:**</u> *"The Lord shall cover you with*
His shoulders. Under His wings you shall find

refuge. His truth shall surround you with a shield."

<u>**Secret Prayer:**</u> *"O' Lord, we solemnly offer You*

our sacrifice at this time of Lent, and pray that by observing abstinence, we may also learn to avoid the defilement of sinful pleasures. Through Our Lord.

The People's Communion Prayer:

"Let my prayer rise as incense before Your sight O' Lord. The lifting up of my hands, like an evening sacrifice."

<u>Post Communion Prayer:</u> *"May the worthy reception of the Blessed Sacrament renew our strength O' Lord, cleansing us from our old selves, and bring us closer to Salvation."*

<u>Dismissal:</u> *"Almighty Father, may these and all the Faithful, nourished by Your Son; the Bread come down from Heaven, continually hunger after You that we may be made worthy of the fullness of everlasting Life, Who lives and reigns forever and ever".*   *AMEN.*

EASTER SUNDAY:

Introit/ Antiphon:

"I arose and am with you still!
Alleluia! You have laid your
hand upon me, Alleluia!
O' Lord, You have proved me
and you know me; You know

when I sit and when I stand.
Glory be to The Father..."

(The Gloria is resumed until Advent)

The Collect: *"O' God Who for our redemption gave Your*
only begotten Son to the death of the Cross, and by His
glorious resurrection delivered us from the power of our
enemy; Grant us so to die daily from sin; that we may

evermore live with Him in the eternal joy of His Kingdom.
Through the same Christ our Lord.   AMEN."

The Gradual: *"This is the Day the Lord prepared, let us*
rejoice and be glad in it! Praise the Lord, for He is good;
His Mercy endures for ever. Alleluia! Alleluia! For
Christ, our Passover, is our worthy sacrifice!"

The Offertory: *"The Earth was silent and in awe when*
God arose in Judgment. Alleluia!"

Secret Prayer: *"Accept O' Lord, the prayers and sacrifice*
of Your people. May the beginning of this
Paschal celebration, through Your Grace,
heal us unto Eternity. Through Christ our

Lord.   Amen."

The People's Communion Prayer: *"Christ our Passover, has been sacrificed. Alleluia! Therefore, let us keep festival with the unleavened bread of sincerity and truth, Alleluia, Alleluia, Alleluia!*

Post Communion Prayer: *"O' Lord, fill us with the spirit of Your love, so that, by receiving this Easter Sacrament our hearts may be united in You, Who is the Glory of the Father, in the unity of the Holy Spirit, one God forever and ever.   AMEN."*

108

Dismissal: *"Go, the Mass is ended. Alleluia, Alleluia!"*

People's Response: *"Thanks be to God, Alleluia, Alleluia!"*

Pentecost Sunday:

Entrance/ Antiphon:

"The Spirit of the Lord has filled the whole world, Alleluia! And That which contains all things has knowledge of His Voice. Alleluia!

Alleluia! Alleluia! Let God arise

and let His enemies be scattered, let those
who hate Him, flee from before Him!
Glory Be…..."   AMEN."

<u>**The Collect:**</u> *"O' God, Who this day instructed the*
hearts of the faithful by the Light of the Holy Spirit,
grant that through the same Holy Spirit we may always
be truly mindful of Him and ever rejoice in His
assuring company. Through Our Lord, Jesus Christ,
Who lives and reigns with You in the unity of the same
Spirit, one God, forever and ever.   AMEN".

<u>**The Gradual:**</u> *Alleluia! Alleluia! Send forth Your*
Spirit and they shall be created, and You shall renew

*the face of the Earth. Alleluia! **(All Kneel)***
Come Holy Spirit, fill the hearts of Your faithful
and kindle in them the fire of Your love."

<u>**The Offertory:**</u> *"Make permanent what You have*
brought about in us O' God; in Your Holy House
let Kings offer their gifts to You! Alleluia!"

<u>**Secret Prayer:**</u> *"Bless our offering O' Lord, and cleanse*
our hearts by the light of the Holy Spirit. Though Christ
our Lord, in Unity with the Father.   AMEN."

<u>**The People's Communion Prayer:**</u> *"Suddenly there came*
a sound from Heaven, as of a rushing mighty wind, and
it filled the whole house where they were sitting, Alleluia!
And they were all filled with the Holy Spirit, and began
speaking of the wondrous deeds of God, Alleluia, Alleluia!"

Post Communion Prayer: *"May the coming of the Holy Ghost, cleanse our hearts, and as heavenly dew, water them to bring forth good fruit. Though Christ our Lord, in Unity with the Father and the same Spirit. AMEN."*

Dismissal: *"May the Holy Spirit, promised of Our Lord proceed continually to be with us at all times, places and circumstances, to enlighten, console, and strengthen His Church, which is the Mystical Body of Christ. AMEN."*

110

Solemnities of The Blessed VirginMary:

Of these two are especially sacred; the Assumption of Mary Aug. 15th, and her Immaculate Conception Dec. 8th. Entrance/ Antiphon: Assumption:

"A great sign appeared in Heaven: a woman clothed with the Sun and the Moon was under her feet, and upon her head was a crown of twelve stars. Sing to the Lord a new song, for He has done wondrous deeds! Glory be to the Father…" Amen.

For Immaculate Conception:

"I will rejoice greatly in the Lord, and my soul

shall be joyful in my God, for He has clothed me with the Garment of Salvation and covered me with the Robe of Justice, like a bride adorned with her jewels. I will extol You, O' Lord, for You have upheld me, and have not let my foes rejoice over me. Glory be ...." Amen.

The Collect for the Assumption: *"O' almighty and eternal God, You have taken up into Heavenly glory the body and soul of the immaculate Virgin Mary, the mother of Your Son. May we always look upward toward Heaven and come to be worthy of sharing her glory. Through Christ our Lord. Amen."*

111

The Collect for Immaculate Conception:

"O' God, by the foreseen merits of the death of Christ, You shielded Mary from all stain of sin and preserved the Virgin Mother immaculate at her conception so that she might become a fitting dwelling place for Your Son. Cleanse us from sin through her intercession so that we also may come to You untainted by sin. Through the same Christ our Lord. AMEN."

The Gradual for the Assumption:

"Hear, O' daughter and see; turn your ear, for the King greatly desires your beauty. All glorious, the daughter of the King enters, clothed in robes spun from gold. Alleluia, Alleluia! Mary was taken up to Heaven; the choirs of angels are filled with joy. Alleluia!"

The Gradual for Immaculate Conception:

"By the Lord the Most High are you blessed O' Virgin

Mary, above all women upon the earth. You are the glory of Jerusalem, you are the joy of Israel, you are the honor of the human race.

Alleluia! Alleluia! You are all fair, O' Mary and there is in you no stain of human tendency to sin. Alleluia!

112

The Offertory: **Assumption:** (Words of God to Satan)

"I will put enmity between you and the Woman, and between your children and her children."

Offertory for: **Immaculate Conception:**

"Hail Mary, Full of Grace, the Lord is with thee. Blessed art thou, among women. Alleluia!"

Secret Prayer: **For the Assumption:**

"Let our gifts, offered to You in devotion, rise before You, O' Lord. Inflame our hearts with the fire of love so that through the intercession of the most blessed Virgin Mary, who was assumed into Heaven they may yearn always for You. Through Christ our Lord.   AMEN."

Secret Prayer: **For the Immaculate Conception:**

"Accept this saving host O' Lord, which we offer You on the feast of the Immaculate Conception of the blessed Virgin Mary. We firmly believe the she was shielded from all stain of sin by Your prevenient Grace; may we be freed from our faults through her holy intercession. Through Christ our Lord.   AMEN."

The People's Communion Prayer: The Assumption:

"All generations shall call me blessed, because he who is mighty has done great things for me."

The People's Communion Prayer:

The Immaculate Conception:

"Glorious things of thee are spoken, O' Mary, for He Who is mighty has done great things for you!"

Post Communion Prayer: **The Assumption:**

"We have received the Sacrament of Salvation, O' Lord and now ask that we may be brought to the glory of the Resurrection through the merits of the intercession of the Blessed Virgin Mary, who was taken up into Heaven. Through Christ our Lord.   AMEN."

Post Communion Prayer: **Immaculate Conception:**

"O' Lord our God, may the Sacrament we have received, heal in us the wounds of that sin from which blessed Mary alone was preserved by reason of her Immaculate Conception. Through Our Lord. Amen."

Dismissal: **Assumption:** *"Through the worshipful prayers of our blessed Mother who after experiencing death was taken body and soul into Heaven by her*

Divine Son, may we ever look forward to sharing life eternal with her in the Glory of His Kingdom.

Though Christ Our Lord Who lives and reigns with the God the Father, in unity with the Holy Ghost, One God, forever and ever.   AMEN."

Dismissal: The Immaculate Conception:

"May the merits and intercession of our incomparable Mother, the blessed Virgin Mary, be ever our help and consolation who was exempted from and kept herself preserved from sin in her Immaculate Conception. Through Christ our Lord."

All Saints Day:

Entrance/ Antiphon:

"Let us all rejoice in the Lord as we celebrate the Feast of

> *All Saints, upon which the Angels rejoice and give praise to the Son of God. Rejoice in the Lord you Just; praise befits the upright. Glory be to the Father…   Amen."*

> **The Collect:** *"Almighty and Eternal God, through Your grace we honor the merits of of all Your*

> *Saints both known and unknown in this single, solemn feast we celebrate today. Grant us the abundant mercy we ask of You through this Army*

of celestial intercessors. Through our Lord Jesus Christ Who with You and the Holy Spirit reigns, one God, from everlasting to everlasting. Amen."

The Gradual:

"Fear the Lord, all you His Saints, for nothing is wanting to those who fear Him. Those who seek the Lord shall not be deprived of any good. Alleluia! Alleluia! Come to me all you who labor and are heavy-burdened, and I will give you rest. Alleluia!"

The Offertory: *"The Souls of the Just are in The Hands of God, and the torment of death shall not touch them. To the unwise, they seem to be dead, but they are in peace, Alleluia!"*

The Secret Prayer: *"We offer these gifts to You in sacrifice O' Lord. May the honor we pay to Your Saints please You, and may these offerings, through your*

116

Mercy, bring us closer to our own salvation. Through Christ our Lord, Who lives and reigns with You in the unity of the Holy Ghost, One God, forever and ever. AMEN."

The People's Communion Prayer:

"Blessed are the pure of heart, for they shall see GOD. Blessed are the peacemakers, for they

shall be called the Children of God. Blessed
are they who suffer persecution for justice'
sake, for theirs is the Kingdom of Heaven."

Post Communion Prayer:

*"May Your Faithful always delight in paying
reverence to all the Saints, O' Lord, and may
the constant intercession of the Saints be our
protection. Through Christ our Lord, Your
Son, Who lives and reigns with You and the
Holy Spirit, God for ever and ever.   AMEN."*

Dismissal: *"Almighty and merciful Father, Who
calls all His children to Holiness and guides
them in the Way of Truth. Go in His Grace and
May the Queen of Heaven and all the Heavenly
Court intercede for us continually."*

117

This Ends the Solitary and Public Mass Rites

Mass Clock

(Mass should be said at all points in

time throughout the world.)

A Prayer before Mass

Eternal Father, through the Immaculate Heart of Mary, I
wish to unite myself with Jesus, now offering His precious
blood (Here name the Country and City) in the Holy
Sacrifice of the Mass for the needs of His Holy Church,
the conversion of sinners, the relief of the souls in Purgatory
and for the special grace I here implore (Speak it).

Solitary Rite of Confession in time of Need

(Composed by Rt. Reverend Vincent Hieronymus Rocha
Bishop and Ordinary of Our Lady of the Rose Cross
Independent Sacramental Church of Evansville, IN. for
the event of the Covid-19 plague which descended upon
us at Lent March 26th 2020. Use if no other priest is
available.) Tuesday, March 31, 2020.

Psalm 51: The Miserere

Have mercy on me, O' God in Your kindness;
Out of Your infinite kindness, erase my offenses.
Wash away my guilt, and cleanse me from my sins.

For I acknowledge that I am a sinner, and I am ever aware

of it. I have disappoint You alone, in Your observing me, and You are right to judge me. Everything has fallen into sin, and from birth, I entered the world through it. But You want honesty and make me to know what saddens You.

Cleanse me with hyssop, that I may be pure; Wash me, that I may gleam more radiant than snow. Let me arise with happy relief; that my depressed body may reach for You in Joy!

Look not upon my sins, but grant me Your pardon. Make my heart pure and strong my God, and make my bond to You everlasting. Do not reject me or withold Your Holy Spirit from me. Grant me once again the joy of Your saving love, and make me obedient to Your will.

I will tell the people who forgot You, all about Your love so that they may remember and return to You.

Save me from Death, that my soul, healed, may praise You forever. Lord, let me not become complacent, with my mouth I will express gratitude. For You do not care about empty promises or gestures. Disinterested worship is not what You desire.

I offer up to You O' God, my broken spirit.

God, mercifully accept my broken, humbled heart. May Your will triumph throughout the World and Your Spirit renew the face of the Earth. Then, You shall graciously receive the sacrifices we make and the offerings we place upon Your Altar.

Glory be to The Father, and The Son, And to The

*Holy Spirit, as it was in the beginning, is now and
ever shall be; World without end.   Amen.*

Prayer before Confessing One's Sins:

*Jesus, my Savior and my God, without You I am nothing.
In Your Gospel, You have taught us to "Ask and you shall
receive", in this confidence, I ask of Your abundant Mercy
to forgive my countless transgressions against Your Sacred
Heart, grant me once more, absolution from my sins and
restoration to Your grace and favor. May I be helped by the
prayers of Your Immaculate Mother Mary, Saint Joseph,
Your chaste foster-father, Saint Michael Defender of all who
trust in You, my holy Guardian Angel, my Patron (name),
and All Your Saints in my struggles toward holiness and on
my journey to rejoin the House of The Father in the Glory
of Your Kingdom forever after.   Amen.*

**(Here, confess all your sins, in a conversational,
honest, and heartfelt manner as completely as possible.
This is contrition.)**

Say an Act of Contrition:

*O' my God, I am sorry for my sins with all my heart.
In choosing to do wrong and failing to do good, I have
sinned against You, Whom I should love above anything.
I firmly resolve, with Your constant help, to sin nor more
and to banish or flee from whatever may cause me to sin*

in my life. Our Savior, Jesus Christ Your Son, suffered and died for us poor sinners. In His Name, my God, have mercy. **Amen.**

<u>Penance</u>

Say Three Our Fathers, Three Hail Marys, and three Glory Be's with the intention of attending to confession again as soon as available, but not to re-confess the sins already spoken in this instance.

or

One may say instead a whole Rosary of five decades for oneself and the conversion of the world.

122

<u>Conclusion:</u> *O' my God, I believe in Thee, I hope in Thee, I love thee, and I adore Thee, and I beg pardon for all those who do not. I wish to be united to Thee in spiritual communion at this time where I cannot partake in person the joyful celebration of Thy Mysteries.* **Amen.**

This rite may be used by priests and laity alike.

<u>For Ordained Priests who must Say Mass after; this prayer:</u>

O' Blessed Virgin Mary, most loving and merciful Mother of the Immaculate Heart and Queen of the most Holy Rosary: I, in shameful unworthiness, a sinner stand before you. From the bottom of my heart,

I ask in your kindness to be my advocate and for the
entire Church who shall receive the Body and blood
of Your Son this day and all days until His return.
As you stood by the Cross of your dying Son, graciously
intercede for me as I approach the Altar of Our Lord,
that I may offer up a worthy and acceptable sacrifice
in the presence of most Holy and undivided Trinity. Amen.

123

Important Prayers

The Our Father:

Our Father, Who art in Heaven, hallowed be Thy Name.

Thy Kingdom come, Thy Will be done, in Earth, as it is in Heaven. Give us this day our daily bread; and forgive us our debts as we forgive our debtors. And lead us not into hard testing, but deliver us from evil.   Amen.

The Hail Mary:

Hail Mary, Full of Grace, the Lord is with Thee!
Blessed art thou amongst women, and blessed is
the Fruit of thy womb; *JESUS.*
Holy Mary, Mother of God, pray for us sinners,
 now, and at the hour of our death.   Amen.

The Gloria:

Glory be to the Father, and to the Son and to the Holy Spirit. As it was in the beginning, is now and ever shall be, world without end.   Amen.

Printed in Great Britain
by Amazon